The Adventures of Sinbad the Sailor

The Valley of Diamonds

Written by Rosalind Kerven

Illustrated by Evelyn Duverne

Ahoy there, you lazy little jellyfish! Do you like adventures?

Well, my name's Sinbad the Sailor and I've come to tell you about my amazing adventures, out on the salty sea. Monstrous birds … treasure … animals wiser than humans … I've seen them all!

Come on, sit down on this barrel. Make yourself comfortable and I'll begin.

Chapter 1

You know, some people just can't be trusted.

Once I was on a ship with a crew that seemed really friendly. When we stopped at a lonely island, they all went off to fetch fresh water.

"We don't need any help from you, Sinbad," they said. "Enjoy yourself. Take a look around."

So I wandered off into the shade of some palm trees. It was very, very hot. I sat down, yawned ... and soon nodded off to sleep.

I woke up with a start and raced back to the ship ...

But it wasn't there.

I had honestly believed that the crew were my friends, but they had sailed off without me. The rascals!

I was marooned.

However, I didn't waste time feeling sorry for myself. Instead, I climbed a tall tree to get a view right across the island.

Way off in the distance, I saw a peculiar white thing, shaped like a dome.

It must be some kind of house, I thought.

I slid down the tree and set off across the island towards it.

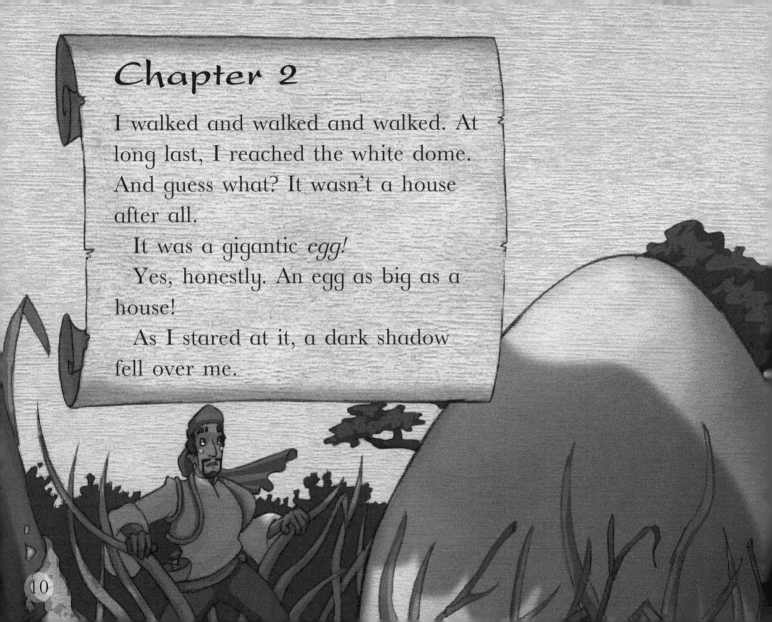

Chapter 2

I walked and walked and walked. At long last, I reached the white dome. And guess what? It wasn't a house after all.

It was a gigantic *egg!*

Yes, honestly. An egg as big as a house!

As I stared at it, a dark shadow fell over me.

It was the egg's mother —
an enormous bird!
I hid behind a rock as
the bird swooped down and
roosted on top of the egg.

11

After much clucking and cooing, the bird went to sleep. And I thought up a brilliant plan to escape from the island.

I unrolled my turban, crept up to the bird, and used the cloth to tie myself to her leg.

When she woke up the next morning, she didn't notice I was there. So she flew away carrying me with her, dangling underneath!

We flew for miles and miles, soaring over land and sea.

At last, we landed in a rocky valley. I untied the turban and set myself free.

As the bird flew away again, I realised I was in worse trouble than ever now. For the sides of this valley were so steep that it was impossible to climb out.

In the bottom of the valley there was a dried-up river bed. Something was glittering in it. I squatted down and discovered that it was full of *diamonds!*

As I stood up, goggling at them in disbelief, I was startled by something hitting me hard on the leg.

I bent down to take a closer look. *Ugh!* It was a lump of raw meat.

Chapter 3

Ah ha! I thought. *There must be diamond gatherers around here!*

You see, when diamond gatherers find a valley like this one, they throw down lumps of raw meat for birds of prey. The birds snap it up – with diamonds stuck all over it. The gatherers catch the birds in their nets and pull the diamonds out of the meat in their beaks. Then they set the birds free, hoping they'll do the same thing again.

Clever, isn't it?

Knowing this, I crammed loads of diamonds into my clothes, then held out a piece of meat. Almost at once, a bird swooped down and snatched the meat in its beak.

As we rose out of the valley, we found ourselves caught in an enormous net – which brought us tumbling down.

The next moment, I was untangled from it by a diamond gatherer. You should have seen the astonished look on his face!

I shared the jewels with him and in return he took me straight back to the coast, where I set sail on yet *another* ship.

But – would you believe it? – this time the ship was captured by pirates!

They seized me as their prisoner and put me in chains for the rest of the voyage.

As soon as we landed in another strange country, the pirates dragged me ashore and into the marketplace. There, a queue of brutish men came up to peer at me, prodding me and arguing with the pirates.

At last, one of them bought me – to be his slave!

Chapter 4

My new master made his fortune by selling ivory elephant tusks. They were turned into beautiful ornaments, which were worth a lot of money.

He forced me to go out hunting and killing elephants. Then I had to cut off their tusks.

I hated doing that, because I love animals.

Of course, the elephants didn't like it either. But they are very wise, and soon found a clever way to stop the hunting.

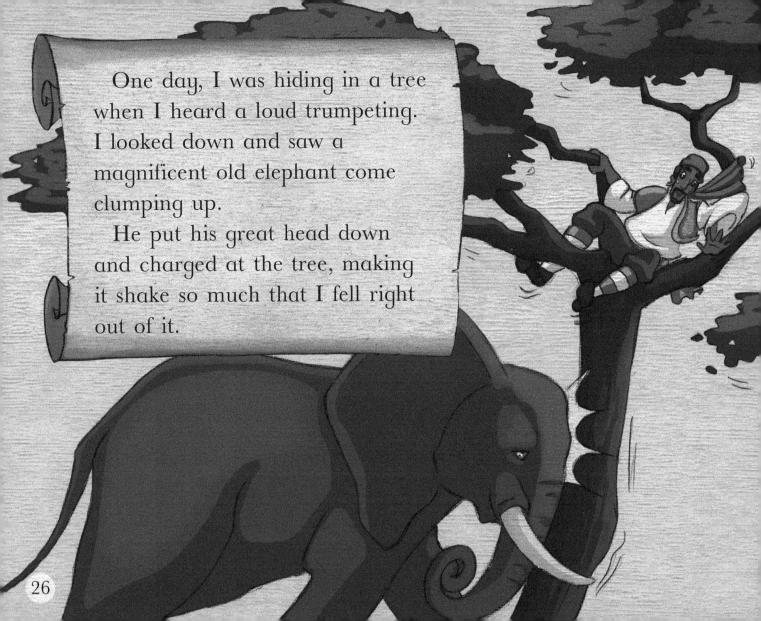

One day, I was hiding in a tree when I heard a loud trumpeting. I looked down and saw a magnificent old elephant come clumping up.

He put his great head down and charged at the tree, making it shake so much that I fell right out of it.

Then, to my great surprise, he gently picked me up in his trunk and carried me away, deep into the wilderness.

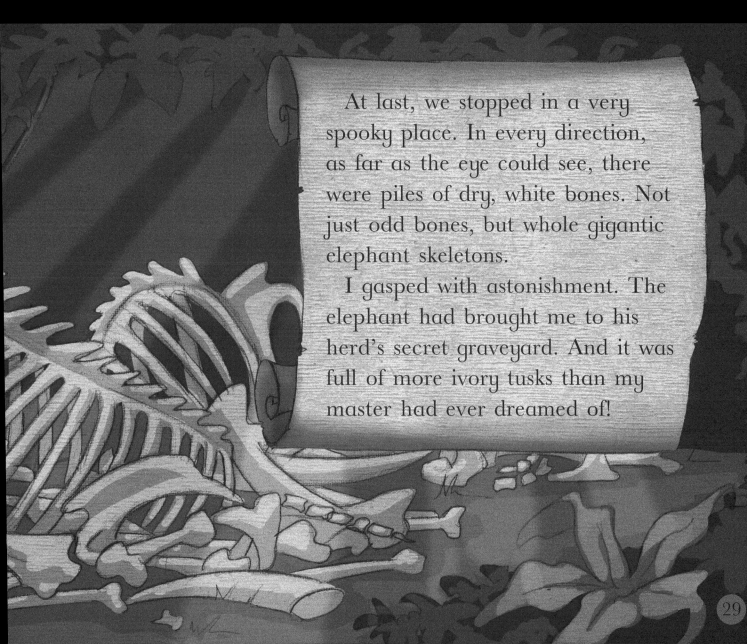

At last, we stopped in a very spooky place. In every direction, as far as the eye could see, there were piles of dry, white bones. Not just odd bones, but whole gigantic elephant skeletons.

I gasped with astonishment. The elephant had brought me to his herd's secret graveyard. And it was full of more ivory tusks than my master had ever dreamed of!

The elephant put me down, nudged me gently and trumpeted softly. I easily guessed what he was trying to tell me:

There's no need to kill us any more. Instead, take as much ivory as you want from here.

I ran back to fetch my master
and took him to see the graveyard
for himself. He was so excited that
he tried to give me a gift of ivory.
But I would not take it, for the only
thing I wanted was my freedom.

So, instead, he booked me onto a ship to take me wherever I wanted to go.

Phew! By seaweed and gulls' wings – I really was free again!